Imagination is Eternity

"Love is the quality of spirit that gives meaning to the movement of time. Love is a gift of eternity. It unites souls that otherwise would be separated."

The Wise Old Dog

www.ChironPublications.com

Interior and cover design by Marianne Green, Sunny Gagliano and Robert LoMascolo.

Printed primariy in the United States of America.

ISBN 978-1-63051-924-7 paperback
ISBN 971-1-63051-870-7 hardcover

Library of Congress Cataloging-in-Publication Data

Names: Blum, David, 1935-1998 author.
Title: Appointment with the wise old dog : bridge to the transformative power of dreams / David Blum.
Description: Asheville, N.C. : Chiron Publications, 2021. | Summary: "David Blum's long-awaited book, "Appointment with the Wise Old Dog: A Bridge to the Transformative Power of Dreams," provides the necessary, comprehensive complement to his highly regarded 1998 documentary. The film, "Appointment with the Wise Old Dog: Dream Images in a Time of Crisis," crystallized his inner work as it related to his cancer experience"-- Provided by publisher.
Identifiers: LCCN 2021010165 | ISBN 9781630519247 (paperback) | ISBN 9781630518707 (hardcover)
Subjects: LCSH: Dreams--Pictorial works. | Dream interpretation. | Dreams--Psychological aspects. | Imagination. | Blum, David, 1935-1998.
Classification: LCC BF1078 .B567 2021 | DDC 154.6/3--dc23
LC record available at https://lccn.loc.gov/2021010165

APPOINTMENT WITH THE WISE OLD DOG

A Bridge to the Transformative Power of Dreams

David Blum

CHIRON PUBLICATIONS • ASHEVILLE, N.C.

TABLE OF CONTENTS

Overture

David Blum

Yo-Yo Ma

Foreword by Murray Stein

A Note by David Blum
A Note by Sarah Blum
Editor's Note & An Invitation to View the DVD

Opus

I Mairi
II Called or Uncalled
III The Play of Opposites
IV Prelude
V The Journey
VI Alfonto's Domain

Coda

In the Mezquita
Dialogue with Alfonto
Mairi's Wedding Song

Endnotes

About the Author
Dreams
Music
Acknowledgments

OVERTURE

David Blum

"It is my hope that the reader will look upon music, as I have experienced it before and during my illness, as a metaphor for his or her own experience.

Each of us has a store of inner gifts.

At a time of crisis or challenging life transition, any powerful image that arises spontaneously from within oneself—in whatever form—brings with it a creative potential.

A friend of mine, a cancer patient, finds precious moments of serenity in conversing with the kindly grandfather, she had known only in her childhood.

That is her music."

Yo-Yo Ma

"The unique paintings David Blum created throughout his life,
and increasingly during his battle with cancer, are a window into his spiritual journey.

The Wise Old Dog, who came to David in dreams, was his guide and comfort.

Through these images and David's insightful commentary, we are reminded
of the resilience of the human spirit, the power of art to help us understand life,
and the role creativity can play in healing and transcendence."

Foreword by Murray Stein

It is an honor to be asked by Sarah Blum to write a Foreword to this work that she has lovingly edited from the diaries and journals of her late husband, David Blum. This book tells a moving story based on the dream records of a gifted man's living and dying (and living), accompanied by brilliantly colored paintings and insightful commentaries. Throughout we hear the music of Beethoven and Mozart sounding quietly in the background.

The reader should be prepared for a deep dive into the life of the soul. The book looks easy at first glance and is fascinating for its colorful paintings (some of them quite humorous and playful), but most of all its significance pertains to the fact that it is a collection of the author's "big dreams" over the course of his lifetime. And these carry a powerful message of revelation of the symbolic levels of the psyche. They reveal, therefore, not primarily the dreamer's personal life history, his complexes and conflicts, but rather the mythological ground of an individuation process that can speak to anyone with ears to hear and the eyes to see. The dreams were a guide and a consolation for the dreamer, and they can serve the same function for the reader who is attuned to their archetypal imagery and symbolic meaning.

David Blum was an internationally acclaimed conductor who followed the patterns and developments in his dreams as carefully as he conducted orchestras through the rhythms and musical unfolding of classical scores by Beethoven and Mozart. In both respects, he resonated passionately to the spirit of the depths. Extraordinarily, he recorded his dreams and carried them with him in steady consciousness from his youth to his death by cancer in his mid-60s. The paintings are further elaborations of his dreams and speak for themselves in the language of form and color. He was as true to his soul as he was to his dear wife and to his musical vocation. Rarely has someone been able and willing to turn such remarkable gifts as David Blum was blessed with, to the purpose of personal psychological and spiritual development. Music and the life of the soul were one for this remarkable man, and he was fully committed to both.

David Blum's story departs somewhat from the usual curve of the individuation process, which generally proceeds in more or less well defined stages from childhood and youth that are dedicated to the promotion of ego development to maturity in the second half of life that is typically dedicated to the realization of the larger self in often spiritual terms. David was gifted with visions and big dreams from an early age, as many people are, but untypically he did not forget about them. Instead, he kept them close in his memory and later recognized their meaning for his life as a whole. The self (in the Jungian sense of the term) claimed him in his teens, and the thread of numinous experiences remained unbroken for the remainder of his life. As he phrases his perception in his commentary on the dream and painting (#24) you can hear throughout this story "an archetypal melody of life."

One may take any one of his paintings and delve ever further into its suggestive symbolic meaning. For example, in "The Venetian Musicians" (#16), which the author places in the series just before he tells us about his fatal illness which was diagnosed some ten years later, we see a black gondola plowing through the waves from right to left, thus moving from consciousness toward the unconscious. The trumpets at the front of the gondola paradoxically "blast forth outwardly," according to the text, while the trombones at the back of the gondola "reverberate their reflections inwardly."

What should we make of this strange reversal? Placing the "outer world" to the left and the "inner world" to the right seems to put them backwards. So where is the gondola headed? It is a picture of introversion. The thrust of the gondola's movement is in the direction of the unconscious.

There is no one in the boat other than the horn players, so one imagines it is going to pick up a passenger in the dark realm of the unconscious, in other words a symbolic content. This signals a movement toward unconscious knowledge of the future, of what lies ahead. What this knowledge is will be revealed in the subsequent pictures. The picture that follows this one in the series is titled "The Reflected Hand" (#17), and the dreamer hears the words: "As below, so above," again a reversal, of the ancient "As above, so below." The heights here mirror the depths, rather than vice versa. It is a symbol of communion and harmony between psyche and cosmos. Obviously, this is the symbol that is needed for the journey to come. The psyche below will tell him about the transcendent world above.

The author reveals that a synchronicity accompanied his dream of the gondola, thus conferring on it archetypal meaning. Of this synchronicity, he writes: "Among the hundreds of synchronistic events I have recorded over a lifetime, this one was particularly astonishing to me. An increased awareness of synchronistic occurrence has given me empirical information about the presence of spirit beyond our normal confines of time and space."

In Venice, the bodies of the dead are transported by gondola to Isola di San Michele, the city's cemetery. There is pomp and nobility associated with the costumes of the music players in this painting. The dream messages in "Venetian Musicians" and the following painting, "The Reflected Hand," prepare the reader for the archetypal process of dying to come. This must have been true for the dreamer as well. The unconscious knows of things that need preparation to be lived authentically and with meaning. It will be a noble death, worthy of a Renaissance prince. The trumpets also announce a future rebirth: It is an annunciation. We have entered the archetypal realm of death and rebirth. The rest of the story is told in the chapters that follow after this one. I chose this painting as an example of how one's mind may follow ancient paths of wisdom by lingering over these dreams and evocative paintings. They open us to the archetypal depths of the psyche. They speak to us, soul to soul.

A Note on
THE DREAM PAINTINGS

David Blum

My collection of paintings represents a lifelong encounter with the pictorial language offered to me by the unconscious. In a sense, during the past thirty-five years, I have been a kind of scribe whose chosen medium has been pastel oil crayons—placed in the hands of my untutored twelve-year-old self. Painting my dreams has been a means through which I enter into the living theater of the collective unconscious* and engage in an inner dialogue with what I call my "peculiar cast of characters" who speak to me in dreams and visions. The auditory visitations, like the dream images, set tasks that my conscious mind often ignores or that are even contrary to my conscious intentions.

The first of my forty-three paintings, *Pastoral Symphony I,* refers back to a 1953 dream I had in Paris when I was seventeen years old. In this dream, Mairi, one of my "cast of characters," proved to be foundational to my life. All that has followed flows from that central experience. Often, I feel Mairi guiding my hand as if she were drawing those universal representations of the psyche's ongoing process of seeking wholeness.

As I become more and more an active participant in the ongoing dialogue with Mairi, the evolution of our lifelong engagement may be traced from *Pastoral Symphony I* through such paintings as *The Harvest* and *I Came, I Saw, I Passed*, to the *Pastoral Symphony II*, that continues in *Garden of the Sea, The Kiss* and *Imagination is Eternity* and finds fruition in *The Sacred Marriage.*

* "[O]ur pictures spring chiefly from those regions of the psyche which I have termed the collective unconscious . . . the source not only of our modern symbolical pictures but of all similar products in the past. It is as if a part of the psyche that reaches far back into the primitive past were expressing itself in these pictures and finding it possible to function in harmony with our alien consciousness." C. G. Jung, "The Aims of Psychotherapy," CW 16, par. 111. Princeton: Princeton University Press, 1954.

In confronting the challenge of how to bring together the archetypal material, an exclusively chronological order seemed restrictive and arbitrary; the inner world is far too rich and replete with nuanced meaning. Rather, I have followed the purposeful patterns and movement of those archetypal dream images as they took shape within me, gathering themselves into a textual and visual format composed of six principal chapters: *Mairi*, *Called or Uncalled*, *The Play of Opposites, Prelude, Journey* and *Alfonto's Domain*. Such a format serves to delineate the flow of unconscious imagery, moving unimpeded in its own time, often within a pronounced circular pattern.

Paradoxically, it has been the cancer experience which has called forth the most recurrent dreams of rebirth, often accompanied by the music of Mozart and Beethoven, music expressive of the utmost calm and courage. In the final chapter, *Alfonto's Domain,* I am guided by The Wise Old Dog towards a full understanding and inner acceptance of the healing process whose goal, in the end, is not confined to getting well physically.

In my writings, there are undoubtedly limitations imposed through the one-sidedness of my conscious attitude. My commentaries are only a hint at the meaning contained in the dreams, and they are certainly not definitive interpretations. The ultimate meaning of dreams perhaps resides in what cannot be articulated, where often words must give way to music. I cannot explain the dreams; rather, they explain me. The dreams are greater than I am; they demand to be recorded and assimilated. My deepest intention is for this work to reveal the healing and redemptive potential of the collective unconscious. My words act, at best, as a bridge to an ever-deeper realization of the transformative power of dreams.

A Note on
APPOINTMENT WITH THE WISE OLD DOG

A Bridge to the Transformative Power of Dreams

Sarah Blum

This improbable book, "Appointment with the Wise Old Dog: *A Bridge to the Transformative Power of Dreams*," elicits intriguing paradoxes. Its *subject* is the psyche, although the author, an internationally recognized musician and writer, possessed no psychological credentials. Its *content* is the distillation of thirty-five years of intensely private, inner work that generated nineteen diaries, six volumes of dream journals, a collection of forty-three dream paintings, and a grassroots movement that resulted in the distribution of more than twenty thousand DVDs. Its *artwork* emerged without the benefit of a single drawing lesson. Its *origin* arose from a personal life-changing conversion in which a self-confessed agnostic, without either psychological or spiritual moorings, was struck dumb by a dream, at the age of seventeen, and found himself on a lifelong pilgrimage towards an experience of the sacred.

What motivated David to take on the task of realizing this improbable book? David hoped his book would provide the necessary, comprehensive complement to his well known 1998 DVD, "Appointment with the Wise Old Dog: *Dream Images in a Time of Crisis*." Profoundly expanding on the DVD, this book contains the *foundational work*–his forty-three dream paintings and commentaries derived from a lifetime of numinous archetypal dreams—so that David's cancer experience becomes only a part of his whole life's story, a coda to his thirty-five year inner journey.

In 1984, after more than two decades of solitary inner work, David entered into Jungian analysis with Dr. Liliane Frey, a close colleague of C. G. Jung, in Zurich. This wise analyst guided him towards a fuller understanding of the symbolic meaning of his dream paintings, thereby supporting his intuitive way of engaging with his dream figures through direct dialogue.

Reaching deeply into his palette—diaries and dream journals—the challenge, as he stated in *A Note on the Dream Paintings*, ". . . is to allow the unconscious imagery to flow, unimpeded." The thematic structure of the book reflects the course charted by the unconscious that moved in a predominantly circular pattern with dream motifs reappearing decades after their first appearance. Nonetheless, a chronological order is also evident in Chapter I, *Mairi,* and

Chapter VI, *Alfonto's Domain*. Within these fundamental thematic structures the images seem to find their meaningful place and interconnection. In his nineteenth and final diary, David writes, "Linking and converging in dreams and waking visions, these archetypal images have shaped my life in known and unknown ways."

David's intention in painting his dreams was not to create "art," but to give form to the elusive images that arose from the depths of his psyche. His paintings were created with a child's spontaneity and audaciousness. Each one took him about five hours, after which he still appeared to be caught up in the dream. When he showed me a drawing, he often expressed surprise at discovering that the dream had continued its story in the appearance of a new character (animal or person), or the deepening of the landscape through structure and color. In essence, David entered into a profound meditative state where the conscious mind no longer inhibits the movement of the unconscious images. Often he lacked all memory of adding to the original dream material. Largely freed of rational control, by re-entering the dream state as he was drawing the image, the dream was free to continue to tell its story.

Music always meant so much to David, a conductor, writer and listener, so that it was natural that music entered into his dreams, significantly deepening the attitude he needed both for the medical challenges he faced and for his whole inner journey. David's living experience of music reached the archetypal reality of the collective unconscious.* Often, music went far beyond the ability of words to realize the meaning of his dreams, visions and active imagination. For David, music was the source of continual inspiration, belonging to his deepest experience of psyche and soul.

* "Music expresses in sounds what fantasies and visions express in visual images. I am not a musician and would not be able to develop these ideas for you in detail. I can only draw your attention to the fact that music represents the movement, development, and transformation of motifs of the collective unconscious." C. G. Jung, *Letters*, vol. 1, p. 542. Princeton: Princeton University Press, 1973.

Among the dream figures in his "cast of characters," the closest to my heart is the companionable Alfonto, David's lovable, childhood, stuffed toy animal; yet this character represents an infinitely greater David as well. In his 1995 diary, David describes something of the meaning carried by Alfonto:

"This simple, frayed and tattered dog, my companion from my sixth year,
whom some would think only fit for the dustbin, acts as my guide and protector.
Alfonto carries the universal wisdom that resides in us all."

Because David would not claim this wisdom as his own, Alfonto speaks with "... a distinctive voice and an archaic turn of phrase." Alfonto, The Wise Old Dog, gives words to David's central vision:

"Love is the quality of spirit that gives meaning to the movement of time.
Love is a gift of eternity. It unites souls that otherwise would be separated."

From his seventeenth year onward, he allowed himself to be guided by those archetypal images, moving inexorably towards their inherent goal of wholeness. In the end, I trust David kept his "Appointment with the Wise Old Dog."

EDITOR'S NOTE

Sarah Blum

The primary sources of David's unedited manuscript are his diaries and journals, dating from his seventeenth to his sixty-fourth year—the crucible into which he poured his most intimate confessions. Though not in David's text, quotations and footnotes—for which I take responsibility—were our shared understanding, and for this reason, I feel they belong. All Jung citations from "The Collected Works of C. G. Jung" are listed as CW. I have used the color magenta throughout for David's voice and chapter headings. My ever-present editing challenge was to bring clarity while sustaining the living spontaneity of the original.

AN INVITATION TO VIEW THE DVD

Accessible on our private (unlisted) vimeo link: https://vimeo.com/420851794

The documentary coalesces word, image and music into a shared, holistic experience of the final phase of David's life journey. The reader is invited to first view the DVD, "Appointment with the Wise Old Dog: *Dream Images in a Time of Crisis*," as a prelude and contemplative pathway into the book.

My deepest intention is for this work to reveal the healing and redemptive potential of the collective unconscious. My words act, at best, as a bridge to an ever-deeper realization of the transformative power of dreams.

OPUS

Mairi

"[E]very man carries within him the eternal image of woman, not the image of this or that particular woman, but a definite feminine image. This image is fundamentally unconscious, an hereditary factor of primordial origin engraved in the living organic system of the man, an imprint or 'archetype' of all the ancestral experiences of the female, a deposit, as it were, of all the impressions ever made by woman. I have called this image the "anima."

—C. G. JUNG

1. Pastoral Symphony I

Dream: *A female figure with streaming golden hair, wearing a Grecian dress, leads me through a field of wheat that sways in the wind to the second movement of Beethoven's Pastoral Symphony. Her extended left hand is not demanding, yet it will not easily be withdrawn. I feel it is my fate to be guided by her. She is simultaneously not of the earth, yet inextricably connected to the earth. Her Greco-Roman features express the masculine intention and energy needed for her present task—to help me fulfill my manhood. The music, the movement of the wheat in the wind, the gold of her hair—they all shimmer like a vision of paradise. I awake bathed in tears.*

Commentary: For a painfully shy, introverted adolescent in his seventeenth year, this dream had the impact of a Pauline experience. The shimmering vision of this Earth-Angel—her oneness with the wind and wheat—is of a blinding beauty. This first painting, Pastoral Symphony I, was drawn ten years after the dream, suggesting in a primitive way something of her knowingness, her resolve. The marvel of her presence vastly exceeded my artistic ability. Over a lifetime, I felt her near me, heard her whispering in my ear, guiding me deeper and deeper into her reality. Instinctively, I understood then that I needed to let her speak freely, that she needed to express herself in any way she wished. For the past thirty-five years, we have been in continual dialogue through word, image and music.

I had no idea then what Mairi's goals were, or the power of consolation she would eventually bring me. She is my rootedness, my daringness to be human, my awakening to nature—both inwardly and outwardly. Over time, I've come to realize that this feminine presence transcends personal experience. Her archetypal image is found in world legends and literature. For Dante, she is Beatrice, leading him from Purgatory to Paradise; Goethe speaks of the Eternal Feminine; Jung of the Anima, the feminine aspect of the soul in man. I had no idea that Mairi was irrevocably setting me upon a path that leads towards wholeness.

She has come to me in dreams in many different transformations.

Pastoral Symphony I (1964), oil pastel on paper, 17.5 x 23.5 inches

2. Mairi of the Rainbow and Sunset

Dream: *Mairi appears as both rainbow and sunset, gradually disappearing into the darkness. Her left hand extends towards me.*

Commentary: Mairi of the wheat field is transformed into Mairi of the sky. Both rainbow and sunset are transitions. The rainbow is a transition that partakes of the wild and the serene. Sunset is that which bridges the two, moving towards the world of darkness. Just as the rainbow hovers for a few minutes in flux, its origin unseen, the sunset spreads wings like an angelic bird that gradually disappears into the darkness. As in *Pastoral Symphony I*, Mairi's left hand extends towards me. I feel bound to follow the movement of the rainbow-sunset, although its origin and destination remain unknown to me. Rainbow and Sunset combine again in subsequent paintings: *The Path of Venus* and *Imagination is Eternity*.

Mairi of the Rainbow and Sunset reappears particularly at times of crisis or watershed moments, as if to reinforce my commitment to follow the Anima's movement towards the depths.

Mairi of the Rainbow and Sunset (1964), oil pastel on paper, 12 x 18 inches

3. Deirdre in the Glen

Dream: *In her traditional Irish red wool skirt, a young girl runs barefoot through the green hills in a lonely Irish countryside.*

Commentary: As I wake from the dream, gripped by the image of the barefoot girl, I ask her to tell me who she is. The answer comes instantly: "I am Deirdre."

I can think of nothing more poignantly moving than the great Irish playwright, John Millington Synge in love with Molly Allgood, working on his play, "Deirdre of the Sorrows," during his last weeks before being brought down by cancer at the age of thirty-eight. The play manifests a spiritual grace rarely expressed elsewhere in literature. Below, Deirdre speaks to her beloved Naisi:

"The dawn and evening are a little while, the winter and the summer pass quickly, and what way would you and I, Naisi, have joy forever? It's a heartbreak to the wise that it's for a short space we have the same things only."*

*John M. Synge, "Deirdre of the Sorrows, Act II," in *The Complete Works of John M. Synge*, p. 237. New York: Random House, 1936.

Deirdre in the Glen (1965), oil pastel on paper, 14 x 16.5 inches

4. Nature's Daughter Rising Amidst Flames

Dream: *From out of deep, flowing waters, Mairi arises like Venus, born from the sea. On either side of the shores, cities are consumed in flames; but behind her the trees still bare green leaves. In her hand she holds the sphere of the world, safe from danger.*

Commentary: Our intervention in Vietnam arouses such indignation within me that it daily draws me out of myself—away from music, away from all inner work. I am desperate to do anything a single citizen could do to change the situation. It depresses me all the more to realize that Vietnam is only one of untold wars of similar brutality which have plagued mankind. The survival of our planet and the survival of humanity depend on our accepting responsibility for the dark side of our psyche.*

The Anima arises from the waters of the unconscious, protecting the outer world from conflagration while bringing her healing power to me as well. Although I cannot ignore the suffering around me, Mairi wishes me to hold my sense of the value of life inviolate from the flames of my passionate moral outrage.

* "The world hangs by a thin thread, and that thread is the psyche of man." C. G. Jung, "The Houston Films" (1957), in *C. G. Jung Speaking*, p. 303. Princeton: Princeton University Press, 1977.

Nature's Daughter Rising Amidst Flames (1965), oil pastel on paper, 13.5 x 16.5 inches

5. The Peruvian Maiden

Dream: *A Peruvian girl resides alone, content to be within her river hut supported by four stilts. Its walls reflect the violet of meditation and the gold of incorruptible value. She bends in a simple ritual towards the bowl. Nature grows in intertwining profusion around the hut. Its stilts are firmly embedded within the river. In this setting, the serpent —a symbol of transformation and inner growth as it sheds its skin and is continually renewed—finds its home.*

Commentary: The girl lives within nature and partakes of it, but as guardian of the soul she has achieved a repose distinct from nature. If she is preparing food, it is surely food of the spirit. Her act of inner reflection embodies a reverence for life. When I listen closely to my Inca companion, whom I call "Maria Latina," I hear her song:

As Solveg never ceased her singing,
though Peer wandered far,
So am I ever singing,
ever awaiting your return.

I came to you first in music,
then in woman,
Then in womanly spirit
to console you, to deepen you.

I dream the depth of your love
that it may never be forgotten.

The Peruvian Maiden (1967), oil pastel on paper, 12 x 18 inches

6. Our Lady of Chartres

Dream: *The Anima weaves herself into the spine of the Cathedral, dedicated to the Virgin, the spiritual core of Chartres.*

Commentary: In Seville during Holy Week on Good Friday, a communal celebration of the living presence of the Virgin begins at about 2:00 am. The "Macarena" (an adored image of the Madonna) is taken on a night journey through the city. Trumpets herald her at every corner and bright lights shine on her gold paint and sparkling jewels. Calling out her name in impassioned "saetas" (arrows of song), the crowd fervently hails the living spirit dwelling within the "Macarena." As dawn breaks, she is carried in triumph into the cathedral.

It becomes all the more meaningful today, when individuals seek to reconnect with their deepest spiritual values, to place oneself in the shoes of those anonymous Gothic artisans inspired by the unifying image of the Virgin.

My life is like a Gothic cathedral. Although I am not part of a medieval community, the age-old experience lives within me. Let me turn from the distractions of modern times and apply myself, like a 13th century man, to the central task of building my cathedral. The stones of my life are interpenetrated by the presence of the Anima. From her meditation arises my architectural being.

She comes in music, in devotion, in love. Mairi builds in stones and dreams.

Our Lady of Chartres (1967), oil pastel on paper, 23.5 x 17.5 inches

7. Gypsies with Staffs

Dream: *A group of gypsies journey by foot through the countryside. They walk between the brown of the earth and the blue of the sky. Their colorful costumes denote the vitality of their beings. Each carries a staff that seems to be leading them.*

Commentary: The gypsies have much in common with Mairi of *Pastoral Symphony I*. They walk toward the left and carry themselves with the same sort of knowing and determination. In their varied ages and characters, they represent Mairi's diverse aspects. They need nothing but themselves. The gypsies are pilgrims, intent on pursuing their own journey. They are a part of nature—cunning, free, humble, yet proud. The gypsy within me says, "Disregard what your instinct does not value." As I was strolling down a deserted Roman street, the images intently playing in my mind, suddenly three gypsy women appeared demanding money. This was a meeting with my instinctive self. The synchronicity* left me shaken.

For more than three decades after having painted the gypsies,
they have led me, often against my will, on the lonely path towards wholeness.

---

* "I chose this term because the simultaneous occurrence of two meaningfully but not causally connected events seemed to me an essential criterion. I am therefore using the general concept of synchronicity in the special sense of a coincidence in time of two or more causally unrelated events which have the same or a similar meaning, in contrast to 'synchronism' which simply means the simultaneous occurrence of two events." C. G. Jung, "Synchronicity: An Acausal Connecting Principle" (1952), CW 8, par. 849. Princeton: Princeton University Press, 1960.

Gypsies with Staffs (1968), oil pastel on paper, 12 x 18 inches

8. Nuns with Torches

Dream: *The nuns or priestesses painted in blue robes carry candles to the transfigured music from Verdi's "La Forza del Destino," Act II, Scene 2—an actual treasured memory from my eleventh year.*

Commentary: Verdi's masterpiece was my baptism into music. These holy women move with determination towards the left, as in the previous dream, *Gypsies with Staffs*. They move towards the unconscious with a definiteness of purpose—a total devotion to their task.

In the same way that I felt called to follow Mairi in the wheat field from my seventeenth year into my sixty-second year, so it was with music, once I came under its spell.

Nuns with Torches (1970), oil pastel on paper, 17.5 x 23.5 inches

Called or Uncalled

Just as images of Mairi have long been with me, images of a masculine deity—Biblical or pagan—have broken through to me in dreams. Some would see these as religious figures; others, perhaps, as archetypes. I cannot answer the question as to whether the essence of what we call God is to be found in some metaphysical region outside of mankind or within the psyche. The dreams for me do not define a binding spiritual conception or conclusion, but rather my own myth with its peculiar cast of characters who move and relate to me—and often set tasks.

9. God Summoned by Mairi

Dream: *I follow Mairi through a tunnel that brings us upwards into the light. A fertile, green valley lies before us. The second movement of Beethoven's Pastoral Symphony infinitely deepens the idyllic serenity. Suddenly there is a fierce rumbling and a black cloud appears like a tornado. I am intensely distressed at this dark apparition. A mighty voice speaks from the tornado:*

"I am the Biblical God. I have come to remind you to always seek Truth."

After these words are uttered, the valley again becomes a scene of bliss. Mairi raises her left hand towards the green valley as she tells me:

"I have brought you to the Land of Love that you may never forget it."

The psyche has subjected me to the fearful, dark side of the Deity. The dream has brought me to a new recognition of the autonomous reality of the collective unconscious and its inherent paradoxical nature—never to be forgotten.*

---

* "[T]he collective unconscious . . . constitutes in its totality a sort of timeless and eternal world-image which counterbalances our conscious, momentary picture of the world. It means nothing less than another world . . ." C. G. Jung, "Analytical Psychology and 'Weltanschauung,'" (1927), CW 8, par. 729. Princeton: Princeton University Press, 1960.

God Summoned by Mairi (1973), oil pastel on paper, 12 x 18 inches

10. God of the Wind*

Dream: *I am rather desperately and ineptly rehearsing Mozart's Symphony No. 25 in G minor, when the whirling entrances of the four string sections to the coda of Beethoven's Leonore III Overture accompany the God of the Wind, pulled by his four horses.*

Commentary: Once again, I am at a rehearsal, feeling acutely disorganized. For me, the rehearsal often represents a metaphor for the psyche's need to integrate inner conflicts. Mozart's symphony, with its balance of dark and light, conveys a path toward integrating the opposites.

There is a state of stillness, of emptiness, in Beethoven's hushed anticipation of the coda. This dream calls for a similar state of receptivity, to be awake and unafraid to welcome this unpredictable force of nature into my life. The finale of Beethoven's 3rd Overture to his opera *Fidelio* embodies the energy summoned by Leonore to liberate Florestan. This incandescent creative energy, personified by the God of the Wind, bursting into the agitation I feel at this moment, delivers Mairi's promise of inner liberation.

He may come in the sweep of a storm, in the flow of music,
in the rapture of love or in the vastness of nature.

---

* "[The god of the wind] seizes everything in its path and overthrows everything that is not firmly rooted. When the wind blows it shakes everything that is insecure, whether without or within." C. G. Jung, *Wotan* (1936), CW 10, par. 391. Princeton: Princeton University Press, 1964.

God of the Wind (1974), oil pastel on paper, 12 x 16 inches

11. Loki

Dream: *I dream of an acquaintance who is the model of civility and refinement. In his place, a naked figure with a green face and wild hair appears, wearing a six-pointed crown of flames. The flames resemble a tree with branches that rise beyond the level of his head. He kneels before a forge, engaged in some ancient ritual, when flames spring up from the forge near his genitals. His hand passes through the fire unscathed.*

Commentary: I have dreamed of the God of the Wind. Now the God of Fire has arisen, the god who visited the Romans, as Vulcan and the Teutons, as Loki. Behind my civilized mask lies a primitive life-force; primordial creative energy that demands an urgent awareness of its power to create and destroy. Fire means not only sex and procreation; it means the warmth of the hearth and ability to cook (the discovery of fire was a cardinal point in evolution). We mortals owe our creativity to that arch-thief, Prometheus. Fire, too, is a particle of that great central power, the sun, of which I have been dreaming.

Loki, what is at the heart of your ancient ritual?
You—with your crown of fire—
an unimaginable force of destruction and creativity.

Is your purpose ultimately to transform
the primordial creative impulse
that threatens to diminish my humanity?

Loki, will I have the moral stamina to follow you,
and kneel before your transformative fire?

Loki (1976), oil pastel on paper, 18 x 12 inches

12. God Shielding the Fruits

Dream: *I see a field with hundreds of apples growing out of the ground rather than on trees. They are imbued with a burgeoning force. An ancient man, wearing a priest-like robe and holding a giant shield, protects the apples so that they will not grow wildly.*

Commentary: The Wise Old Man,* guardian of the Anima-energy, tends Mairi's creative force so that it will not become self-destructive. Recently, I observed the eminent Swiss conductor, Ernest Ansermet, conducting Debussy's *Pelléas et Mélisande*, nourishing the work's inner beauty with a similar mixture of sublime care and loving caution manifested by The Wise Old Man.

He who protects the fruits of life
brings a patient wisdom that counterbalances,
but in no way denies Loki's fire.

---

* "With further differentiations the figure of the (wise) old man becomes detached from the anima and appears as an archetype of the "spirit." He stands to her in the relationship of a "spiritual" father, like Wotan to Brünhilde . . . " C. G. Jung, " VIII. The Sacrifice," CW 5, par. 678. New York: Pantheon Books, 1956.

God Shielding the Fruits (1978), oil pastel on paper, 9 x 12 inches

13. God and the Golden Coffin

Dream: *Out of my golden coffin, I am taken into the hand of God.*

Commentary: My golden coffin lies on the watery shore; it has been drawn up from the sea. I lie on top of the coffin. The depth of my feeling has arisen—no longer lost in projection—and I reach out to the Deity. As I am taken into God's hand, I am struck by an overwhelming recognition of the supreme value of the inner process that began in my seventeenth year, and of the deepening awareness of my connection to the infinite.*

*A psychic shift is taking place towards fully accepting archetypal reality
and participating in its ongoing purposefulness towards wholeness.*

---

* "The decisive question for man is: Is he related to something infinite or not?" C. G. Jung, *Memories, Dreams, Reflections*, p. 325. New York: Pantheon Books, 1961.

God and the Golden Coffin (1980), oil pastel on paper, 16 x 19.5 inches

The Play of Opposites

"The possibility of progress, of achieving knowledge of what we are, lies in the tension between opposite states of mind, not in their resolution by one gaining supremacy over the other."

—WILLIAM BLAKE

14. The Lantern

Dream: *There appears a softly glowing, four-sided Chinese lantern, each side decorated with images of myself and the Anima. These words come to me:*

"The Lantern is like a dream. You must study a dream through each of the four sides of the lantern. Take care, when looking through one side, that its light shall not mingle with the light coming from the opposite panel. Then, after you have viewed the dream through each separate panel, you may look over the top—down into the lantern."

I obey. When I look over the top, I see within the lantern ruby-red blood in a perpetually boiling cauldron.

Commentary: *The Lantern* balances the play of opposites. Its panels represent the four points of Jungian orientation to inner and outer realities: intuition, feeling, thinking and sensation. The ruby-red blood is a traditional symbol of the soul, something I did not learn until some years after the dream.

I tend to view life from the standpoints of intuition, feeling, and sometimes thinking, while ignoring sensation. Given my introverted and intuitive nature, I will always be in the process of refining my orientation to external reality. When I looked, so to speak, through the sensation panel, the light shed by the other functions blurred the image. Even though I hated to turn away, even momentarily, from the seductive filters of intuition and feeling, the dream asks me to look into the four panels separately, independently and not let the light of the lantern fuse with the light of the opposite panel; only when this task is realized may I see the whole from above. The four points of orientation in Jung's typology have become a living experience rather than an abstraction, resembling a string quartet where the four voices are both differentiated and integrated.

The Lantern (1986), oil pastel on paper, 17.5 x 23.5 inches

15. Angels and Thieves

Dream: *A voice says*:

> "When you have a red light
> It shall be placed among the thieves;
> When you have a green light
> It shall be placed among the angels;
> When you have both
> They shall be placed side by side, and used wisely."

Commentary: Regardless of the years of intense psychological work on the shadow side of my personality, I am aware of it operating in my daily life. On the other hand, my evolving consciousness of the shadow's presence has perhaps kept me from the inflation of identifying with being an entirely "good person."

The unconscious sets before me the life-long task of becoming a balanced person, aware of the simultaneous presence of thieves and angels (the dark and light within my psyche), and to use them wisely.*

---

* "[T]he deeper down the level of consciousness goes, the more you are threatened by the unconscious. . . . But, if you can just keep afloat, you have accomplished that task; then you will land somewhere in between . . . in the middle, between the perfect and the imperfect bodies. You would expect it to be among the perfect bodies, but the perfect bodies are up on the conscious level and that is not the real middle position." C. G. Jung, *Nietzsche's Zarathustra*, CW I, pp. 479 - 480. Princeton: Princeton University Press, 1935.

Angels and Thieves (1982), oil pastel on paper, 12 x 18 inches

16. The Venetian Musicians

Dream: *I see a gondola in which four musicians clothed in Renaissance garb are playing golden instruments. Two trumpeters face the front and two trombonists face the rear. The four instruments sound simultaneously in opposite directions to hold the boat in balance. The image is accompanied by these words:*

> "The trumpets blast forth outwardly
> While the trombones reverberate their reflections inwardly."

Commentary: As the gondola glides with uncanny motion over the waves, partaking of the deep, music expresses itself in energy and repose. Every outer task must be complemented by an inward one. Renaissance is brought about by the balance of opposites.

The same day I drew *The Venetian Musicians*, I happened to look, for the first time, through a book of photographs of Roman orchestral instruments and came upon a photo of an ancient Roman wall painting which depicted a mosaic of two seated trumpeters and two seated trombone players. Among the hundreds of synchronistic events I have recorded over a lifetime, this one was particularly astonishing to me.

*An increased awareness of synchronistic experience has continually
informed me of the presence of spirit beyond our normal confines of time and space.*

The Venetian Musicians (1984), oil pastel on paper, 12 x 18 inches

17. The Reflected Hand

Vision: *The hand stretching towards the sky is reflected in the water. I hear the words:*

"As below, so above."

Commentary: I am viscerally shaken by this waking vision that, with the utmost of simplicity, depicts a reconciliation of conscious and unconscious. This unifying image of the opposites releases the necessary psychic energy to forge a new attitude.

While contemplating those four words enunciated by the dream, I am reminded of past images that contain four as the ancient numerical symbol of wholeness* reiterated in: *God of the Wind, The Lantern and The Venetian Musicians.*

This dream is a beneficent preparation for the crisis to come.

* "Although "wholeness" seems at first sight to be nothing but an abstract idea (like anima and animus), it is nevertheless empirical in so far as it is anticipated by the psyche in the form of spontaneous or autonomous symbols. These are the quaternity or mandala symbols, which occur not only in the dreams of modern people who have never heard of them, but are widely disseminated in the historical records of many peoples and many epochs. Their significance as *symbols of unity and totality* is amply confirmed by history as well as by empirical psychology." C. G. Jung, Aion, vol.9 II, par. 59. New York: Pantheon books, 1959.

The Reflected Hand (1986), oil pastel on paper, 13.75 x 16.25 inches

Prelude

It's an amazing fact that at a time of dire crisis, people often unexpectedly find themselves supported by a power quite beyond their ordinary experience that makes it possible for them to cope. Any powerful image that arises spontaneously from within—no matter how irrational it may seem—carries a creative potential. I had such an experience when at fifty-two my cancer was first diagnosed. I knew that the situation was serious, and I was frightened. I had support from my wife, Sarah, my family and my friends; but support also came from an unexpected quarter. Recently, my beloved, long-haired dachshund Papageno died at the age of sixteen. Strangely enough, he now came back to me in a dream.

18. The Dachshund String Quartet

Dream: *Papageno and three other dachshunds enter a church in a forest, take up stringed instruments and play Beethoven's Quartet No. 13, in B flat major, IV. Alla danza tedesco. On the back wall, within the musical notation of the movement's opening theme, there is a window in the shape of a mandala.**

Commentary: Beethoven's Quartet brings me a deep reassurance in this time of trouble. I made this picture of the dream in the enthusiastic way I used to draw when I was twelve. When one is faced with a life-threatening illness, one is fearful, as a child might be fearful. Sometimes it's best to counter such fears with child-like means.

During every medical procedure, I enter into their church in the forest where
The Dachshund String Quartet plays for me Beethoven's Quartet, this music of health and joy.

---

* "It is an age-old symbol that goes right back to the prehistory of man. It is the symbol of wholeness. . . . I am not whole in my ego; my ego is a fragment of my personality. The center of a mandala is not the ego, it is the whole personality . . ." C. G. Jung, "The Houston Films" (1957), in *C. G. Jung Speaking*, pp. 327, 328. Princeton: Princeton University Press, 1977.

The Dachshund Quartet (1987), oil pastel on paper, 17.5 x 23.5 inches

19. The Golden Eagle

Dream: *Mairi appears at my bedside. She gives me two dappled eggs she had taken from a golden eagle. From each of the eggs a golden child is hatched. One is named "waves" and the other "wings." Energy flows forth from these children, consisting of all that is most beautiful in human feeling. Throughout the dream I hear the Finale of the Pastoral Symphony, Mairi's music.*

> *David:*   *Now, Mairi, we enter upon a new phase of our journey together.*
>
> *Mairi:*   I speak to you David, my dearest, blending my solitude with your solitude, so that we shall never know aloneness. Let wings unfurled embrace us both. Let the sea of our deep eternal feelings embrace us both. We are forever protected when we are together.
>
> *David:*   *Forever means longer than life, Mairi. Am I destined to end this life soon?*
>
> *Mairi:*   Forever is in every moment. Therefore, life is spirit, and spirit is eternal.

Commentary: This dream came to me the night before my first operation. In the painting, there is a controlled flow of energy in the form of a triangle, beginning with its tip at the sun and enlarging as it passes through the eagle, Mairi and the newborn children, until it finds its base just above me. The eagle is a primal force of nature—revered and admired in many cultures. The letter A in Egyptian hieroglyphics is represented by the eagle, standing for the warmth of Life, the Origin, the Day. The eagle's natural energy and the spiritual protection of Mairi are a tremendous combined force. The golden children bring newborn life.* If the blessing of a helpful spirit could be conveyed spontaneously to someone in deep dread, it was conveyed by Mairi on that night.

---

* "[T]he fountainhead can only be discovered if the conscious mind will suffer itself to be led back to the "children's land," there to receive guidance from the unconscious as before." C. G. Jung, "Individual Dream Symbolism in Relation to Alchemy: Introduction" (1944/1952), CW 12, par. 74. Princeton: Princeton University Press, 1969.

The Golden Eagle (1987), oil pastel on paper, 16.5 x 23.5 inches

The Journey

While the doctors were trying to assess my condition, the dreams are ignoring the outer situation and setting their own agenda. I am simultaneously undertaking two journeys: one medical, the other spiritual. The movement of unconscious energy that directs me is not chaotic, but purposeful. It only seems chaotic when my conscious mind is not harmonized with my wandering—not trusting to the movement of energy in the dream world, even if it sometimes seems random and fragmented.

20. Vézelay

Dream: *I find myself on a spiritual pilgrimage, beginning at the church of Vézelay in France. Alfonto, the faithful hound of the dream, and Sarah, the eternal helpmate, are in attendance. To the music of Wagner's "Good Friday Spell," Parsifal proclaims me Knight of the Grail. I am tasked with traveling over the face of the earth in search of my own Grail, with my hound following faithfully at my side. My crusader's boat sets sail, leaving the great ranges of mountains and verdant valleys.*

Commentary: Surrounded by megalithic stones, a forest and a simple village, the Romanesque church of Vézelay sits high on a hill overlooking the fertile Burgundian countryside. On the seaward side of the church, a crusader's ship awaits me. I envision, in the center of the church, my own Grail— the ultimate goal. With a sense of Parsifal's vision and purpose, I embark on my spiritual pilgrimage.

As my crusader's ship sets sail, the sublimely inspired music of redemption
from the final scene of Parsifal carries my spirit onwards towards its life's quest.

Vézelay (1992), oil pastel on paper, 16.5 x 23.25 inches

21. The Eskimo Poem

Dream: *I am a solitary boatman set adrift. The second movement of Mozart's String Quartet No. 15 in D minor, accompanies me on my journey, sounding the dream's inexpressible mystery. I find myself drawing a rainbow that arches above me, in which I place the words of an anonymous Eskimo poem:*

"The great sea has set me in motion,
set me adrift.
And I move as a weed in the river.

The arch of sky and mightiness of storms
encompass me.
And I am left trembling with joy."

Commentary: Immediately after setting down the poem, images arise accompanied by words. I listen.

*Twilight gradually settles over a small French fishing village
at the edge of the Mediterranean.
The brilliance of the sea now takes on a quiet depth.*

*The water beats upon the shore, infinitely renewed from Roman times,
since Dido's tears soaked into the waves.
A Phonecian fishing boat sails by. Listen to that quiet lapping.*

*We are an ongoing part of a whole. We know not
where it leads; but a part we are—if only we would listen.*

The great sea has set me in motion, set me adrift, and I move as a weed in the river.
The Arch of sky and mightiness of storms encompasses me
And I am left trembling with joy

The Eskimo Poem (1988), oil pastel on paper, 16 x 19.5 inches

22. The Harvest

Dream: *I walk along a sunlit path to a village square where rustic merrymakers are celebrating the festival of the harvest, which dates back to the Middle Ages. I am standing in Mairi's wheat field. Farmers are carrying bundles of wheat, and in the village square, jugglers are displaying their skills. The first movement of Beethoven's Pastoral Symphony, Awakening of Happy Feelings upon Going into the Country, is heard throughout the dream. I am overwhelmed by this earthly sublimity and awake to the following words:*

"The wheat cannot be threshed by the wind;
It must be threshed by the mind."

Commentary: This dream comes at a time of fulfillment: the young man who, at seventeen, dreamed of following the Anima through the windblown fields, has now learned how to communicate with her—to live into Mairi's depth of feeling, to accept her and be accepted by her. Within the wholeness of the village square, I enter into an age old ritual of harvesting the soul's ripe wheat field. In the threshing process, the self* becomes the new reality—its inner goal, beyond all goals. Beethoven's *Pastoral Symphony* is the music of celebration from which Mairi, the Madonna of the pagan earth, draws herself cradling a new-born infant. I am that child.

I stand in awe before the promise of this wondrous birth.

---

* "[T]he self is our life's goal, for it is the completest expression of that fateful combination we call individuality. . . ." C. G. Jung, "Two Essays on Analytical Psychology," CW 7, par. 404. Princeton: Princeton University Press.

The Harvest (1990), oil pastel on paper, 17.5 x 23.5 inches

23. Z

Dream: *I am walking through an Italian village called Folia. This town of winding streets and ocher buildings is poor and forgotten. There is a great highway stretching above its entire length. I wonder why the city dwellers cannot create a park and greenery instead, so that they can come into the sunlight and establish a place of social gathering. As I am pondering these questions, an image flashes like a bolt of lightning at the end of the highway—the letter Z, with a little rectangle raised at the top—startling me with its living presence.*

Commentary: I have often dreamt of villages in Portugal and Italy, wandering within those wonderful, circular, mandala-like structures. As I begin to paint my neglected dream village, I feel an irresistible need to realize something of its reconstitution. The colors of my painting are not the pale ocher in the dream, but vivid dark blues and violets which, together with the gold of the highway and arches, convey a luminosity, even a spirituality. The inhabitants of this strangely stylized Mediterranean or Arabic village have not yet emerged; however, the houses themselves, with their oval or diamond-shaped windows looking towards us, seem almost to resemble people.

Folia has musical resonance. "La Folia" is an old dance tune of Portuguese origin. Its vital harmonic structure has formed the basis for innumerable variations, notably by Corelli. For me, it has a quality of ancient inevitability, of haunting and imperishable beauty.

The dream asks me to become conscious of what is beneath the "high-way," rather than blithely sailing over it. My task is to delay my journey until I have looked downwards to rehabilitate the forgotten community and integrate it into the stream of my life—to find Folia's ". . . vital harmonic structure. . . ."

In 1993, nearly two decades after the dream, Sarah and I visited Ravenna. While studying the magnificent sixth-century mosaics in the church of San Vitale, I saw a solitary Z prominently inscribed on Christ's robe. In 1975 I had written in my diary: "I must search for the meaning of Z." When I asked our guide about the choice of the letter, she explained that the Greek letter Z stood for the Greek word Zoe, meaning "eternal life." For an instant, the letter Z at the end of the golden highway flashed before me, startling me with its living presence—perhaps even more intensely than when it had first appeared two decades before.

Z (1975), oil pastel on paper, 16.5 x 23.5 inches

24. I Came, I Saw, I Passed

Dream: *I walk by a row of restored Venetian palaces, one of them a theater—not the largest or most lavish, but my own theater, taking its modest but rightful place on the historic street, which is one of the loveliest in the world. As I awake, I hear the following words paraphrasing Caesar: "I Came, I Saw, I Passed" (rather than "Veni, Vidi, Vici," it has become "Veni, Vidi, Abii"). I am following in the direction of the celestial hand. The whole of Mozart's Piano Concerto No. 27, in B flat major weaves through the dream.*

Commentary: "Veni, Vidi, Abii" summarizes my present transition *from* "I Came, I Saw, I Conquered" *to* "I Came, I Saw, I Passed." I have experienced the world, but don't need to conquer it. The ego can retire. It is the self that prepares me for the unknown by continuing to reveal the patterns of my interior life experience, shaped by the cast of characters who reside in my theater. In the painting, Mairi offers guidance, but significantly, from behind. I seem to know my way; she only wants to be sure that I do. We both are moving toward that celestial hand which appears from time to time at critical transitions, much like the hand of God in the sixth-century mosaics of *St. Apollinaris in Ravenna*.

*The opening theme of this Mozart Concerto has the quality of leave-taking,
a theme which is related to the composer's acceptance of death as a friend.
The dream finds completion in this archetypal melody of life.*

I Came, I Saw, I Passed (1994), oil pastel on paper, 16.5 x 23.25 inches

25. Journey with the Monk

Dream: *Sarah and I find ourselves in a village in the heart of the Italian countryside. A Franciscan monk shows us his farmhouse, from which a large cow resembling an Assyrian carved relief comes forth. The monk then leads me up along a solitary hillside. The path winds upwards to the summit where I discover a monolith in the shape of a white pyramid with an Egyptian inscription which reads, "The journey will be radiant." I cry out to the monk in amazement, "Is this reality, or only a dream?" The monk confidently leads me on. I descend alone to the cave-like manger, (where the Madonna and Child reside with the cow), and ultimately return to the baptistery.*

Commentary: This dream-journey takes the Judeo-Christian faith back to its Egyptian origins. The boat that awaits me is reminiscent of the Crusader's vessel in the Vézelay dream. The Crusader's boat took me into life, while the Egyptian boat will take me beyond life, along the eternal flow of the Nile.

While I was working on the painting, images that were not in the dream painted themselves, as if they were a natural extension of the dream. The first of these was *The Baptistery of Parma** at the beginning of the path; the second, the Madonna and child, living in a cave-like manger, which they share with a cow. The unconscious traces a circular pilgrimage, beginning and ending with the baptistery, as the spirit is reborn and sustained. The child will need to be baptized; the journey will begin again. The outer and inner structure of *The Baptistery of Parma* expresses the perfect form of a mandala. Its art-work, in its child-like naiveté and faith, is imbued with a divine grace.

Now that I no longer needed to conquer life, perhaps I was ready to become a novitiate.

* "Churches and holy places frequently appear in my dreams, most prominently in the following dream paintings: *Our Lady of Chartres, The Dachshund String Quartet, Journey with the Monk, God Will Act, Ocean Vision* and *The Sacred Marriage*." David Blum, Diary XVIII, 1997.

Journey with the Monk (1994), oil pastel on paper, 17.5 x 23.5 inches

Alfonto's Domain

We all know of fairy tales in which an animal mysteriously appears to help the protagonist out of danger at a critical moment. Alfonto led a peaceful life on a shelf for half a century, but after my cancer recurrence, he began to come into my dreams, guiding me and speaking to me in a distinctive voice with an archaic turn of phrase.

In my sixty-second year of life, a down-to-earth person, neither seer nor mystic, I was being spoken to and guided by my stuffed toy animal. Though I consider myself a modern skeptic without religious preconceptions, the dream images and visions that accompany Alfonto's reappearance convey such power that they leave me in no doubt as to their autonomous, timeless reality. With an instantaneous knowingness, I recognized Alfonto as the indispensable catalyst and guide—The Wise Old Man, who first appeared in dream #12.*

* "[T]he wise old man appears in dreams . . . in the shape of a man, hobgoblin, or animal where insight, understanding, good advice, determination, planning, etc., are needed but cannot be mustered on one's own resources. The archetype compensates [for] this state of spiritual deficiency by contents designed to fill the gap." C. G. Jung, "The Phenomenology of the Spirit in Fairytales" (1945), CW 9. I, par. 398. Princeton: Princeton University Press, 1968.

26. God Will Act

Dream: *I am alone in the midst of a mountain valley. To my amazement, I hear Alfonto's voice:*

"Trust, and thou shalt not be alone."

I kneel in prayer. From far off, a motorcyclist of death comes roaring towards me. Alfonto appears, raises a golden spear and says, "God Will Act." With Alfonto's pronouncement, the opening Allegro measures from Mozart's Adagio and Fugue in C minor, accompany the instant destruction of the motorcyclist. The Hand of God descends from the clouds. The notation in the river is Mozart's String Quintet in G minor.

Commentary: The dream has chosen *Mozart's String Quintet in G minor K. 516* with uncanny wisdom; it seemed natural that the work's opening theme appear in my river. The music is a perfect metaphor for the attitude I need in facing my ordeal. Mozart's work hovers between light and dark. No expression of genius more tellingly depicts the fragility and wonder of life than in the introduction to the Finale where sorrow stands in juxtaposition with joyous affirmation, a joy that co-exists with the darker forces of human destiny.

"God Will Act"—what a grand concept, but could I believe in it? After all, I hadn't any idea who or what God may be, or whether God exists at all? And on whose authority was I accepting this pronouncement? That of a toy dachshund! Yet it seemed inherently right to follow my childhood animal unquestioningly when he comes on my behalf to battle the forces of chaos.

Alfonto speaks directly to my fear of death. In life, one can risk dying spiritually—through fear or depression—in an hour, a day, a week. I've since come to accept that the wonder of Alfonto's statement "God Will Act," is that it can be interpreted on many levels.

God Will Act (1994), oil pastel on paper, 17.5 x 23.5 inches

Last night, I had a dream in which I was told that I had an appointment at 1:15pm with Alfonto, The Wise Old Dog. When I awoke, I wondered: Why on earth 1:15pm? Then, I realized that this was the appointed time for a crucial MRI exam, so that when I entered the machine, it was less as a medical patient than as a friend of the old dog.

27. The Dachshund Valley

Vision: *Once inside the MRI, I let the conscious mind dissolve into the imaginative world. A Swiss village appears entirely inhabited by dachshunds. At mealtime each day, Alfonto sets the menu of roast beef, chicken, leg of lamb, meatloaf, hamburgers, wine-veal stew or turkey and the dogs dine together at a long table in a beautiful hall. Sick dogs are tended by loving dachshund nurses. At night the great Mother Dachshund comes down from the starry sky and spreads her ears over the valley to protect any dog that is ill and afraid.*

Commentary: Once the image of the hounds appears, the scene unfolds naturally and with remarkable detail. The image of the sleeping hounds in their blue baskets has more than once eased my anxiety before a crucial scan. Whenever I have difficulty sleeping, Sarah tells me that I am a dachshund in one of the soft blue baskets, and I gradually sink into slumber.

The Dachshund Valley (1995), oil pastel on paper, 17.5 x 23.5 inches

28. The Winged Alfonto

Dream: *I kneel before a totem pole, although I do not know why I am genuflecting before it. I feel that this gesture honors the animal spirit—lion, fox, bird, fish and dachshund. Alfonto is elevated to the skies, endowed with the golden wings of an Evangelist. Covering his entire chest is a mirror in which Mairi is reflected, walking through wheat fields as in my first dream at the age of seventeen. To the music of the second movement of Beethoven's Pastoral Symphony, she points the way towards the pyramid and sun, and the pyramid appears just as in Journey with the Monk.*

Commentary: I am amazed to see Alfonto—now, in the shape of my childhood dachshund Papageno—raised to the skies, this hound who normally keeps close to the earth. I have no recollection of adding the wings of an Evangelist. Mairi's right hand points towards the sun and the pyramid. At this time of crisis, Alfonto comes to me in the fullness of his power, carrying the image of my soul in his magic mirror. Alfonto and Mairi, each in their own way, challenge me fully to accept death, informing me of my readiness.

Before I can accept their challenge, medicine intervenes in the form of a surgical biopsy. The cancer was found at last, but in a place that was inoperable. We decided to use my lifetime limit of additional radiation.

The Winged Alfonto (1995), oil pastel on paper, 17.5 x 23.5 inches

One morning when I found myself alone in my hospital room, undisturbed, I thought this would be the time to accept Alfonto's challenge to step into the magic mirror. The question was: How can a hospital room turn into a wheat field?

29. Pastoral Symphony II

Vision: *I begin conducting Mairi's music. Mairi appears. We wander arm in arm through the fields. Sarah is there, too. Then with amazing ease, Mairi lifts me above the valley. At first I hold on to Sarah's hand; but as I am taken higher into the sky, I am forced, against my dearest wish, to let go of it. This is unbearably painful—so painful that, at first, I am unable to draw it. As Mairi and I glide among the clouds, I feel burdenless, without anguish. But it isn't time yet for me to leave the earth. She takes me back down to the fields. Mairi then tells me that just as the medical radiation infiltrates my body, her radiation infiltrates my mind. She lets the intense rays of her light pass into me. I am bathed in her luminosity, shaken to the core of my being.*

Commentary: All of Mairi's movements are inspired by the flow of Beethoven's music, its wondrous, mysterious modulations and melodic tenderness. I continue to let the music flow through me, tears streaming down my cheeks. I let them come. Sarah and Mairi sing the theme from the *Pastoral Symphony, II. Andante, molto moto*, played in different keys by the oboe, clarinet and flute. Every phrase brings consolation. I feel permeated by each of these feminine spirits.

As Mairi takes me back down to the fields, I am left with a new and deepening acceptance of death. The medical radiation has come and gone, but hers remains.

The Pastoral Symphony II (1995), oil pastel on paper, 17.5 x 23.5 inches

30. The Two Moons

Dream: *I am standing backstage at the Royal Concertgebouw in Amsterdam when Herbert von Karajan enters for his rehearsal with the Berlin Philharmonic. For a moment, his eyes turn in my direction, his gaze hovering in detached, pale luminosity. Two moons suddenly appear over a vast ocean—the eyes of a man looking entirely inward.*

Commentary: This dream comes to me just at the moment when new, frightening medical challenges appear. Recently, I have had several nightmares in which I must go down a steep ladder into a dark cave. How to find the courage?

When this great Austrian conductor closes his eyes while conducting, he removes himself from the outer world and enters into a trance-like altered state of consciousness, becoming one with the music.

In the painting the eyes look inward, like jewels over the vast ocean waves,
their shimmering light releasing the life energy needed to enter into the cave.

The Two Moons (1997), oil pastel on paper, 16 x 19.5 inches

31. Ali Baba's Cave

Dream: *In the foreground of Ali Baba's Cave, I find the frightening, familiar ladder descending into a deep pit. This time, I ask Alfonto to be my guide. He wears golden wings about his ears to light the way and tells me that we are going to climb down the steep ladder. He pleads with me not to be afraid. Knowing that I have to go down into that cave, I put my trust in Alfonto and follow him.*

Commentary: The cave in my dream holds some of the life long treasures that I love most: the musical scores of the great composers; the writings of Jung; the greatest literature, beginning with Dostoevsky and Chekhov; all the Madonnas of Raphael. . . .

Ali Baba's Cave (1995), oil pastel on paper, 7.25 x 10.5 inches

32. Madonna of the Grotto

Vision: *With Alfonto leading the way, still wearing his evangelical wings, I find myself trustfully following him into a mysterious grotto where he takes up his spear and points at the dark sky. A swirl of golden light emerges in which Mairi and her child reside in all their simple majesty. Alfonto and I converse:*

Alfonto:	She is waiting to illuminate your inner journey.
David:	*Yet, how can she enter into my life? She is transparent and I am concrete.*
Alfonto:	When she reveals herself to you, you become more transparent and she, more concrete; you thus share in each other's worlds.
David:	*How will I know that she will be there for me in a moment of peril?*
Alfonto:	Acceptance cannot reject.

Commentary: The many dreams of a mother and child insistently point the way toward "rebirth"—some sort of continuation of spirit beyond life. The question is not whether I "believe" in rebirth, but what the dreams have to say. And the dreams had something extraordinary to say about rebirth when my cancer began to spread significantly after six months of stability. In the midst of our anguish and despair, Sarah and I decided that our only true course was to trust Alfonto and Mairi to guide us.

In the week after our frank acceptance of death, a whole
series of dreams on the renewal of life presented themselves.

Madonna of the Grotto (1995), oil pastel on paper, 17.5 x 23.5 inches

33. The Path of Venus

Dream: *Mairi arises as Venus from her shell, transforms herself into a rainbow and bequeaths the dew of her love to mankind until disappearing into the night, only to be born again the following day. Alfonto is there, too, in the shape of a constellation among the stars. I am the small figure in a boat in the midst of the sea. I ask Alfonto:*

  David: *What is the circle of time?*

  Alfonto: The circle in which your imagination roams freely.

  David: *How can I get there?*

  Alfonto: By following the route to nowhere.

Commentary: I do not recall drawing either the boat or myself—a miniature figure confronting the vast starry universe. In this dream I am now fully contained within the circular rainbow of Venus, the Goddess of Love. Her path, a revivifying circumambulation through dark and light, death and rebirth, can be conceived in different time dimensions: over the course of a day, of a lifetime, of an existence beyond life. Her energy is ever-replenishing.

The 6,000-year-old megalithic tomb stones we saw at the site of Almendres in Portugal have signs of stars carved into them, patterned after the visible constellations. Alfonto's constellation and the markings in the stones, glistening like stars, suggest cross-currents of energies cast over vast fields of time and space. They focus and vitalize me in my brief moment of life.

When I die, these great forces—the circular journey of Venus through water and sky, the pattern of the stars—will not disappear. And their presence will permeate my spirit, in whatever form it may take.

The Path of Venus (1996), oil pastel on paper, 23.5 x 17.5 inches

34. Sunset and Sunrise

Dream: *I stand with Sarah on a rock in the middle of the ocean, with simultaneous views of the sun as it rises and sets.*

Commentary: The two suns, east and west, form a circle around the earth. To witness the complete cycle of nature's renewal is a vast thing! The rock upon which we stand provides a vantage point infinitely wider than our ego. The sun does not set without also rising. Life joins death which joins life again. So the great circle moves us. Life lives its ever moving circle through us.

In the crisis we now face, Sarah and I can do nothing better than to stand together on our rock in mid-ocean and experience nature's replenishing circle not only in the context of twenty-four hours, but in the larger context of "life" and "death." We have different tasks to perform. Mine is to let go of life; hers is to hold onto it. From the dream's central vantage point, we can understand that letting go* and holding on are not opposites.

The spirit is a continuum; it does not end—it transforms. If we comprehend the true nature of our journey, we can undertake it hand in hand.

---

* "Not for nothing is this "letting go" the *sine qua non* of all forms of higher spiritual development, whether we call it meditation, contemplation, yoga, or spiritual exercises." C. G. Jung, "A Study in the Process of Individuation" (1933), CW 9.1, par. 562. Princeton: Princeton University Press, 1968.

Sunset and Sunrise (1996), oil pastel on paper, 12 x 18 inches

35. From Lascaux to London

Dream: *I am one of the prehistoric animals painted on the cave walls of Lascaux in France: a horse with the antlers of a deer. Beethoven's Symphony No. 7 in A major—that ecstatic paean to life—reverberates throughout the sanctuary. I venture forth from the cave to have a look at the modern world, ambling down London's Regent Street, doing no one any harm, yet people respond to me with some consternation.*

Commentary: One of the principal benefits of knowing that your life will end soon is to act on your desires. Sarah and I had longed to one day visit the original cave of Lascaux, the Sistine Chapel of prehistoric art. We both knew now was the time to go down into mankind's ancient sanctuary.

When I descended into the cave and saw its walls and ceilings covered with astonishing paintings of animals, I felt swept along by a tremendous life force. What first struck me, what took my breath away, was the wall painting of five deer, one having just plunged into the river, the other four eagerly waiting to make their river crossing. Recently, I dreamt of having to ford a river. This 20,000 year old image revealed the meaning of my dream! I am waiting my turn with those remaining four deer still on the shore—waiting, with joyful anticipation, to make the final crossing.

The dream sanctuary tells me all I need to know at this crucial hour when I am suspended between time and timelessness. As the body becomes more limited, the spirit expands. An animal-spirit has been activated within me, moving me onwards—powerfully, inevitably, even joyously—despite my frailness of body. At the end of all, I've turned into a prehistoric horse-deer.

Cro-Magnon man's dreams and images have walked into my dreams and I have walked into his. This secret correspondence offers me deep solace in confronting my coming transition, harmonizing my soul with something eternal, and flooding me with energy that sweeps away my frailty.

Let me live with the image of those five deer—confident, joyous, enthralled—
submitting to the river's flow, doing gladly what must be done.

From Lascaux to London (1996), oil pastel on paper, 17.5 x 23.5 inches

36. Garden by the Sea

Dream: *Sarah and I wander among the 18th and early 19th century gray shingled houses of Nantucket, when we find ourselves in front of an idyllic garden by the sea. Mairi comes to me as a black-haired Roman girl. I embrace Sarah and Mairi as the second movement of Mozart's String Quartet No. 19 in C major holds the three of us in its embrace. I ask Alfonto:*

David:　　*How can my love of Mairi, who will soon take me into her arms, also protect Sarah when I am gone?*

Alfonto:　　Mairi is greater than David. Her love penetrates him and becomes his love of Sarah. Thus, David and Sarah will always be together.

Commentary: While Sarah and I are both still in temporal life, we are united in the spirit world, perhaps more so now when the unconscious prepares us for our final farewell. There are a hundred subtle and telling ways in which our spirits converse with one another daily. When I die, I shall enter entirely into the spirit world where Sarah's spirit—waking or dreaming—will continue to intermingle with my spirit. Thus, we shall be together in our *Garden of the Sea*.

Garden by the Sea (1996), oil pastel on paper, 23.5 x 17.5 inches

37. The Kiss

Dream: *A waterwheel appears, its axle combining past, present and future time. Alfonto is overseeing the shifting of time: his task is to replenish the axle, moving the wheel clockwise. The water splashing from a bucket onto the axle is Spirit—a power of revivification—the source of which derives from a region beyond our temporal perception, transcending time. Alfonto's words resound over the splashing water:*

**"Love is the quality of spirit that gives meaning to the movement of time.
Love is a gift of eternity. It unites souls that would otherwise be separated."**

A deer drinks from the stream, reminding me of the marvelous Roman mosaic in the Basilica of San Clemente— the soul thirsting for God. I ask Mairi:

David:	*Why must I endure so much pain and grief?*
Mairi:	Ask not why you must endure it, but how you endure it. Be prepared in sorrow and in faith.
David:	*How can I know that in death, I shall not fall into a void?*
Mairi:	Foolish boy, don't you know that the "reality" around you is merely a preparation for the greater reality? These stones will crumble; these trees will die; this sky will change—all you see will disappear, but I shall remain. How can I forsake thee when I am the truest being thou hast ever known?

Commentary: Everything in the painting, aside from the axle of the wheel, stands outside of time as we generally know it. The task set before me, whatever suffering I must endure, is to hold the vision of Mairi's world with my last breath.

My fear of death has been put to rest.

The Kiss (1996), oil pastel on paper, 17.5 x 23.5 inches

38. The Wheel

Vision: *I see a vast, wooden wheel that turns in all ways, at all times, and in all places. The wheel has nine spokes between which float nine planets. The wheel spins; the planets move within the spinning wheel.*

Commentary: Light glows from the center of the wheel—an inner solar system. The nine planets vary in color and distance from the center, as the wheel ceaselessly turns. All of life turns like a wheel. Relationships are fashioned from the energy created by overlapping wheels of friendship and love. One need only join the twilight corso in an Italian town to sense the energy of this harmonious motion. When I conduct a concert, the orchestra, the audience and I are encompassed within a wheel, with its central energy flowing from the imagination of the composer. The earth rotates; the self moves in a perpetual circular pattern. Yet, we often resist submitting to the larger rhythmic patterns of which we are a part and tend to cut time into convenient slices of the here and now.

The dream asks me to participate in life in an unbroken way. It asks me to explore the inseparable correspondence between the inner and outer, between aloneness and togetherness, between the limitation of our life's moment and our timeless continuity with the oneness of creation.

What power created this ageless archetypal wheel, set it in motion, turning in all ways, in all times and in all places? Whatever that power may be, it also fashioned Alfonto's wheel in The Kiss.

The Wheel (1997), oil pastel on paper, 17.5 x 23.5 inches

39. Maui Vision

Vision: *As the sun sinks into the sea, Alfonto wields his magic spear, turning the sun's golden rays into an amber city—Yeats's Byzantium, Blake's Jerusalem, Baum's City of Oz—beneath the waves. Alfonto whispers to me. "Penetration to depth creates imperishable gold."*

A simple Mediterranean village harmoniously spirals up to its church. Mairi with her child awaits my arrival. Suddenly, from the dome of the sky, the hand of God descends as a blessing. All is enclosed in a mandala shaped rainbow. The waves speak:

"Do not resist. Enter into the amber city. Accept our protection.
You have no choice but to do gladly that which must be done."

David:	*Why is it that despite the complexity of life, the simplest things carry one's truest experience?*
Alfonto:	Simplicity prefigures eternity.
David:	*How can I compare my earthly joy with the unknown yet to come?*
Alfonto:	The unknown holds the key to the box of treasure.
David:	*Could the box be empty?*
Alfonto:	Not if the heart is full.
David:	*When will my earthly existence end?*
Alfonto:	It has already ended. Thou hast stepped onto the bridge.
David:	*The waves flow on. Must I depart, joining them in the endless unknown?*
Alfonto:	Unknown to thee; Known to God.

Maui Vision (1997), oil pastel on paper, 17.5 x 23.5 inches

40. Etruscan Tomb

Dream: *This Etruscan tomb is my burial tomb. The interior contains two stone beds opposite each other, one for Sarah and one for me. At the foot of my bed a basket is prepared for my dachshund, Papageno, and above us the Anima blessedly protects us. I envision wonderful frescoes capturing scenes of banquets, wrestling, horse-riding, erotic games, fishing, swimming, birds, dolphins, seahorses and leopards from the Necropolis of Tarquinia painted on the barren walls within my tomb.*

Commentary: At the Necropolis, Sarah and I visited seven burial chambers, most of which dated from the 6th or 5th centuries BC. I was entirely incapable of recreating those frescoes in my painting, but could clearly visualize them in my dream. These astonishingly beautiful frescoes present a paradoxical juxtaposition of movement with repose.*

Beside the ever-flowing river, priestly cypresses spring from the outer, green-clad tumulus, affirming fertility in the presence of death. Amphorae stand ready to receive provisions for the long journey. The images—sealed in solitude and darkness for 2500 years—generate the courage and inner strength I now need to economize and apportion my energy.

*Glowing from within the entrance shines a golden light,
the inner sun—a wondrous gift from the unconscious.*

---

* "For me, the slow movements to Beethoven's *Archduke Trio,* Mozart's *Symphony No. 29* and the *Clarinet Concerto,* along with the rising scale of the violas toward the end of the *Tristan und Isolde Prelude*, are the musical embodiments of Etruscan repose." David Blum, Diary XIX, 1998.

Etruscan Tomb (1997), oil pastel on paper, 17.5 x 23.5 inches

41. The Ruby-Rose

Dream: *Deep within the earth lies a great Celtic Cross. In its center is a glowing ruby enclosed within a rose.*

The Ruby-Rose speaks:

"I am at the center of aloneness
that penetrates to the depth—rooted in the earth.

I am enclosed within my petals,
yet embracing and bequeathing the radiant energy of love,
while needing to be watered.

Love that penetrates to the depth—creates the incorruptible value."

*Neither words nor music come to me as I meditate on this image of wholeness.
The Ruby-Rose calls out for Tacita, the Roman Muse of Silence.*

The Ruby-Rose (1997), oil pastel on paper, 12 x 18 inches

42. Imagination is Eternity

Dream: *Mairi and I stand at the edge of a vast, flowing river. She wears the same traditional Irish red peasant wool skirt and black shawl that she wore when she came barefoot in my dream, thirty years ago, as Deirdre in the Glen. We stand face to face—our foreheads touching. Blake's words, "Imagination is Eternity," among the other curving lines of land, river and sky. The curve of this phrase is infinite.*

Enfolded in Mairi's spirit of replenishment, my finite existence in time and space finds completion within the infinite curve of imagination.

Imagination is Eternity (1997), oil pastel on paper, 16 x 19.25 inches

43. The Sacred Marriage

Dream: *I find myself in a mosque that unifies the architecture of the great Moorish mosques in Cordoba and Granada. A marriage ceremony is taking place inside the mihrab. The couple perform a sacred marriage rite—an ancient dance resembling one of Alhambra's immeasurable geometric patterns. The dancers are reflected in the water. Alfonto, who draws himself in my painting with two heads, gives me instructions on how I may fully participate in the sacred marriage.*

> "Hold fast to Mairi's transparent grasp,
> Fulfill your sacred duty as Bridegroom,
> Let the Way of Love penetrate your being."

Commentary: This painting, derived from both a dream and a vision, interpenetrated my experience of the two great Moorish mosques. The ceiling of the sacred niche, where the marriage ceremony takes place, appears as a three-dimensional mandala; its core has flame-like rays, and comes as a spontaneous inner event, taking the form of light and energy. The worshipper, bowed in prayer, experiences the gift of silence.

Sometime after the painting was completed, I learned that Janus, the Roman god, is represented with a double-faced head, each face looking in the opposite direction—god of future and past, gates and doors, comings and goings, beginnings and endings, transitions and thresholds.

Alfonto, now cast as the god of transitions, a carrier of the opposites, becomes my trusted guide on my own transition towards the threshold of death. Holding fast to Mairi's transparent hand, filled with the joy of the dance, I step over the threshold.

The Sacred Marriage (1997), oil pastel on paper, 17.5 x 23.5 inches

CODA

Taken from *The Sacred Marriage* (1997), oil pastel on paper, 17.5 x 23.5 inches

"The ceiling of the sacred niche, where the marriage takes place, appears as a three-dimensional mandala; its core has flame-like rays, and comes as a spontaneous inner event, taking the form of light and energy."
—*David Blum*

Having walked a long time with the aid of my cane through the forest of arches, and now quite tired, I ask Sarah to go on for a little while without me. On a bench within the great interior of the Mosque, I remember taking out my pocket notepad and hurriedly trying to set down the following verses, for the most part dictated by the voice of the columns.

In the Mezquita

I am the voice of the columns.
My voice is great, but locked in stone.

We are Staffs of Life—like your cane.
We absorb your joys and sorrows.
We have known greater sorrows than thee.
We are questions perpetually asked.

What slaves have carved us, fashioned us, erected us?
What is our voice, locked up in stone?
Where is our soul, encased in polished marble?
Why have we stood together through the ages
    Rooted in Carthaginian plain or Roman forum?

We hold the temple from collapse:
An army of the soul's need,
A forest of contemplation,
An oration of Seneca,
A meditation of Maimonides.

We march with you, my child, through Eternity.
We come to the Holy City of Byzantium.
We measure your fragility with our strength.
We are black with Wars.
We are red with Love.
    Each different,
    Each guarding his own secret.

Sing the Ancient Song,
    The song that belongs to the centuries.
Sing the Temporal Song,
    The song that tells of joy and woe.
Sing the Holy Song.
    We are arched in prayer.
Sing the Silent Song,
    The song of wholeness.

Those who sense our secrets
    Dare not speak.
Those who love as we have loved
    Can only whisper.
Those who dare to witness that to which we strive,
    Can stammer at best.

Alfonto and Mairi speak to me, one following the other, as if the theme of my conversation with Alfonto—the quest for meaning in the transition to death—is answered by Mairi's Wedding Song.

Dialogue with Alfonto

David: *Will my staff be as strong as these columns?*
Alfonto: Stronger yet, for thy living spirit supports thee.

David: *But, when I must say farewell to life. . . ?*
Alfonto: There is no farewell, but eternal welcome.

David: *Where is the Mihrab of my faith?*
Alfonto: Thy faith is arched over thee.
         It encompasses the mightiness of storms.

David: *I am but a grain of dust in the midst of infinity.*
Alfonto: Spirit knows no measure. Love knows no measure.
         Partake, my child, and thou shalt know all.

David: *I need courage to be alone in the forest.*
Alfonto: Alone is Together.

David: *My life is but one little column.*
Alfonto: All is connected.

David: *What shall I do in my remaining time?*
Alfonto: Know the connections.
         Have joy in them.
         Triumph in them.
         They will bring you nothing at all—
            But wisdom.

Mairi's Wedding Song

David: *Now give me your hand.*

Mairi: Thou hast it. The most transparent grasp is the firmest of all.
No earthly force can separate it.

David: *Mairi of the wind: who or what is the Maker before whom the two of us,*
stumbling together, must kneel?

Mairi: We kneel before the life in Raphael's brush,
Before all of the faltering, palpitating themes of Bach,
The Eternal Flux of Heraclitus, before Alfonto's Wisdom.
Our Maker is the Energy of Eternal Love.
To no other would I bend my knee.

David: *Help me submit.*

Mairi: Embrace me, kiss me, stumble with me.
Before thou knowest it, we shall stumble together—
before the throne of God.*

*The entire CODA was written, in one sitting, in the Mosque of Cordoba. David Blum, Cordoba, Spain, 1997. (ed.)

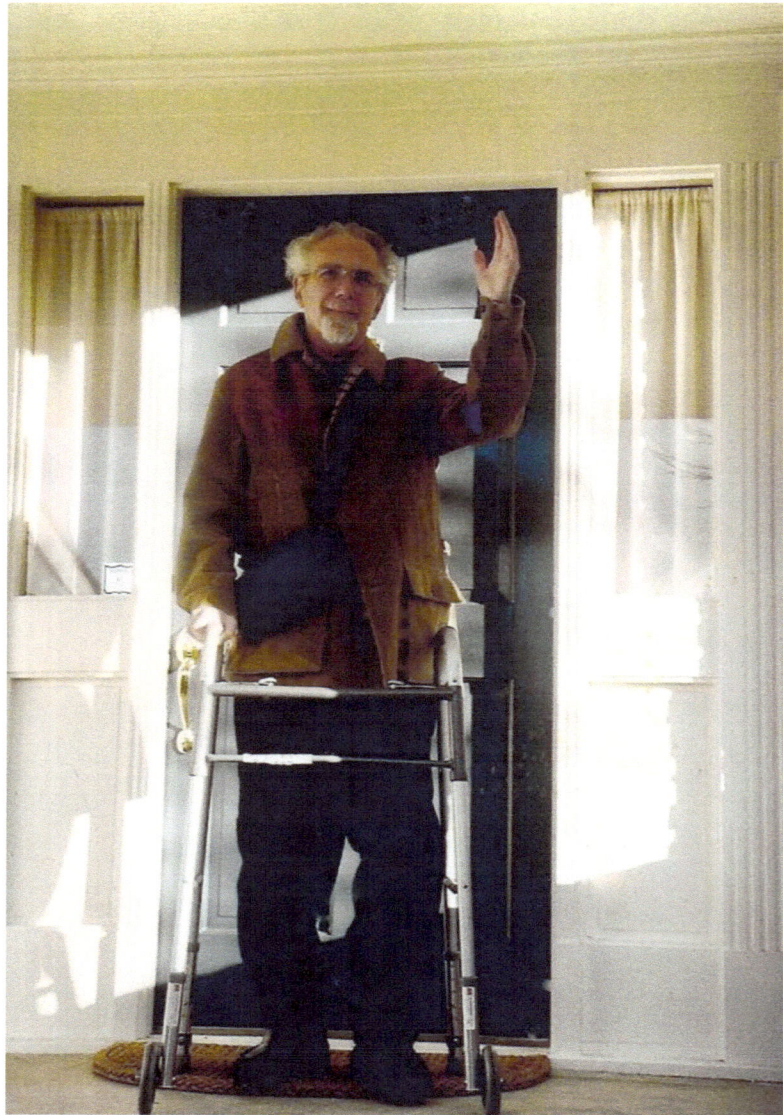

One of the fearful aspects of death is its vast autonomous power; but the dreams and visions have an autonomous power of their own. I feel that I'm meeting death with some measure of equality. But is it death? Shelley wrote:

"Death is the veil which those who live call life;
They sleep, and it is lifted."

A friend recently tried to reassure me that miracles are always possible. I said that I'd gladly accept one, but doubted that one would take place. Then I caught myself and said:

In fact, a miracle has taken place.

David Blum

September 7, 1935 - April 17, 1998

ENDNOTES

About the Author

The following excerpt is taken from The London Times obituary of May 1998:

David Blum leaves an extraordinary musical legacy as conductor and writer. He studied composition and conducting at the Juilliard School of Music. In his early twenties, he recorded with the English Chamber Orchestra and guest-conducted throughout Europe, America and Israel. His meeting with Pablo Casals at the 1953 Prades Festival was a transformative experience and one which not only informed his music-making ever afterwards, but also led to a close friendship with the legendary musician that was to last nearly two decades.

In 1961, David founded The Esterhazy Orchestra in New York, with Casals acting as Honorary President. Dedicated to the music of Haydn, the orchestra gave groundbreaking tours throughout the U.S. and Canada. The acclaimed series of recordings of Haydn symphonies on the Vanguard label permanently preserve the remarkable collaboration between David and his outstanding musicians.

In the 1970s, and over the next two decades, David became an esteemed writer on music and musicians, frequently contributing major articles for The New York Times, The New Yorker, the BBC Music Magazine and The Strad. His books, which have been translated into many languages, include: Casals and the Art of Interpretation, Paul Tortelier, The Art of Quartet Playing, and Quintet.

As a writer, he revealed the inner working approaches of some of the greatest performers of our time. Although he was a prolific writer, he could only ever write about those artists with whom he felt a passionate empathy, and whose genius became woven into the fabric of his own life.

The great sea has set me in motion, set me adrift, and I move as a weed in the river.
The Arch of sky and mightiness of storms encompasses me
And I am left trembling with joy

Dreams

I Mairi

1. *Pastoral Symphony I*
2. *Mairi of the Rainbow and Sunset*
3. *Deirdre in the Glen*
4. *Nature's Daughter Rising Amidst Flames*
5. *The Peruvian Maiden*
6. *Our Lady of Chartres*
7. *Gypsies with Staffs*
8. *Nuns with Torches*

II Called or Uncalled

9. *God Summoned by Mairi*
10. *God of the Wind*
11. *Loki*
12. *God Shielding the Fruits*
13. *God and the Golden Coffin*

III The Play of Opposites

14. *The Lantern*
15. *Angels and Thieves*
16. *The Venetian Musicians*
17. *The Reflected Hand*

IV Prelude

18. *The Dachshund String Quartet*
19. *The Golden Eagle*

V The Journey

20. *Vézelay*

21. *The Eskimo Poem*

22. *The Harvest*

23. *Z*

24. *I Came, I Saw, I Passed*

25. *Journey with the Monk*

VI Alfonto's Domain

26. *God Will Act*

27. *The Dachshund Valley*

28. *The Winged Alfonto*

29. *Pastoral Symphony II*

30. *The Two Moons*

31. *Ali Baba's Cave*

32. *Madonna of the Grotto*

33. *The Path of Venus*

34. *Sunset and Sunrise*

35. *From Lascaux to London*

36. *Garden by the Sea*

37. *The Kiss*

38. *The Wheel*

39. *Maui Vision*

40. *Etruscan Tomb*

41. *The Ruby-Rose*

42. *Imagination is Eternity*

43. *The Sacred Marriage*

Music (referenced in the dreams and heard on the DVD)

Dream 1. Pastoral Symphony I
Beethoven Symphony No. 6 in F major, Op. 68, II. Andante molto moto.

Dream 8. Nuns with Torches
Verdi La Forza del Destino, Act II, 2nd scene.

Dream 10. God of the Wind
Mozart Symphony No. 40 in G minor, K. 550, 1st movement
Beethoven, Leonore III Overture (coda).

Dream 18. The Dachshund String Quartet
Beethoven String Quartet No.13 in B flat major, Op.130, IV. Alla danza tedesca.

Dream 19. The Golden Eagle
Beethoven, String Quartet No.15 in A minor, Op. 132, III. Molto adagio,
"Heiliger Dankgesang eines Genesenen an die Gottheit, in der lydischen Tonart."
Beethoven, Symphony No.6 in F major, Op. 68, V. Allegretto (Finale).

Dream 20. Vézelay
Wagner Parsifal, "Good Friday Spell."

Dream 21. The Eskimo Poem
Mozart String Quartet No. 15 in D minor, K. 421, II. Andante.

Dream 23. Z
"La Folia," a traditional Portuguese dance tune.

Dream 24. I Came, I Saw, I Passed.
Mozart Piano Concerto No. 27 in B flat major, K. 595, I. Allegro.

Dream 26. God Will Act
Mozart Quintet No. 4 in G minor, K.516
Mozart Adagio and Fugue in C minor, K.546.

Dream 28. The Winged Alfonto
Beethoven Symphony No. 6 in F major, Op. 68, II. Andante molto moto.

Dream 29. Pastoral Symphony II
Beethoven Symphony No. 6 in F major, Op. 68, II. Andante molto moto.

Dream 34. Sunset and Sunrise
Mozart Quartet No. 15, in D minor, K. 421, II. Andante.

Dream 35. From Lascaux to London
Beethoven Symphony No.7, A major, Op. 92.

Dream 36. Garden by the Sea
Mozart String Quartet No. 19 in C major, K. 465, II. Andante Cantabile.

Dream 40. Etruscan Tomb
Beethoven Archduke Trio in B flat major, op.97.
Mozart Symphony No. 29 in A major, K. 201.
Mozart Clarinet Concerto in A major, K. 622.

Acknowledgments

In the two decades it has taken for this book to be born, wise guides and helpers appeared throughout the birth process. The first three characters appeared as if out of a Hans Christian Andersen fairy tale: Yo-Yo Ma, June Singer and Marion Woodman bearing their quintessential gifts of vision and trust.

Yo-Yo, my thanks are given, in Beethoven's words "from my heart to yours," for your two wonderful expressions of trust in David's inner life. The first was your moving introduction to David's DVD, made more than twenty-two years ago, and the second, your present eloquent appreciation of his book. In both instances, you acted before there was confirmation from the public or commitment from a publisher. Your trust was a blessing then and is a blessing now.

June and Marion, I carry the image of you as beneficent fairy godmothers who intuitively recognized that out of the volumes of diaries, dream journals, unpublished manuscript and forty-three dream paintings, there was a book waiting to be realized—a book that would be a significant contribution to Depth Psychology and that would still be fully accessible to the general public. Your initial vision and trust resound throughout the long birthing process and beyond.

To you, the many thousands of viewers of David's DVD, "Appointment with the Wise Old Dog, *Dream Images in a Time of Crisis,*" who have reached out to me with your personal letters, emails and phone calls, I bow my head in gratitude before your precious sharing. It was your need for David's foundational work, the rhizome beneath the DVD, which became a central source of my motivation. Your affirmation of David's healing work is, in large part, the reason for this book.

Joe Kulin's tireless efforts led to the generous Donald Rubin Grant that made possible the preservation of David's paintings as well as the creation of the digital reproductions in this book. To you, Joe, my enduring thanks.

Two years ago, Marianne Green, a beloved friend, naturally assumed the role of midwife—a most wished-for partner in the birthing of this book. Marianne's own profound experiential connection with David's interior journey deepened her remarkable capacity to understand and to enter into his dreams. Marianne, how do I thank you for your unconditional readiness to accompany me in our relentless struggle to know and to fulfill David's intentions while maintaining astonishing patience, grace and humor? This book would not have been realized without you. Thank you, Marianne, for your incomparable contribution.

We were not alone. A small community of readers and wordsmiths began to gather around us—all magnetically drawn by the work and unanimous in their generosity. Each of you contributed something essential. My thanks to Audrey Bernstein, Ardan Michael Blum, Pamina Blum, Steve Buser, Joan Cenedella, Kelsey Cheshire, Kathy Elliott, Sunny Gagliano, Sarah Gauger, Reto Gieré, Vicki Halper, William vanden Heuvel, Mollie Moore, Betsy Neisner, Marc Paquin, Judy Skenazy, Maxine Schmidt, Robert Speck, Barbara Svoboda, Fran Volkmann, Grace Bakst Wapner and Jerry Wapner.

For their help in all theoretical matters, I am indebted to three extraordinary Jungian analysts: Bette Joram, Russell Lockhart and Dennis Merritt. Each has lived with David's psychological legacy over decades.

Bette, my close friend and friend of the book, your remarkable musical ear and brilliant mind—ever clarifying and refining—remain a significant part of this work. I am deeply grateful.

Russ, you are among David's supremely wise guides; no one has both understood his inner work and acted on its behalf more fully than you. Your connection with this book lives longer than life. Our thanks.

Dennis, thank you for your constancy of support and unfailing helpfulness over these many years. As a prolific writer, your literary input has been invaluable.

And then, there are Evangeline Glass and Melinda vanden Heuvel, each of you walking beside me on that yellow brick road, where your love and support provided the courage to enable me to realize this book. Our transformative journey together has led me to this place of deepest thanksgiving.

Finally, we have come full circle from the vision and trust of those two beneficent fairy godmothers at the beginning of our tale to the realization of Murray Stein's vision and trust in this newborn book. And it is your Foreword, Murray, that has released this book to journey into the soul of the reader, "soul to soul." In the spirit of a fairy tale ending, David and I thank you with gratitude that endures "forever after."

—*Sarah Blum*

www.ingramcontent.com/pod-product-compliance
Lightning Source LLC
Chambersburg PA
CBHW040317270326

41929CB00004B/32